WHAT IS "SPIRIT?"

PASTOR AL GEE

Copyright © 2024 by Pastor Al Gee.

All rights reserved.
No part of this book may be reproduced or used in any manner without written permission of the copyright owner except for the use of quotations in a book review.

Unless otherwise noted Scripture references are from the King James Version of the Bible.

Book Project Management by
Raindrop Creative, Inc. | StartWrite Publish Team

Editors:
Gerald C. Simmons, Tiara Brown

Cover Art:
R. Davis

2nd Edition Print

ISBN: 978-1-970179-21-7

Table of Contents

Table of Contents 3
Foreword 5

Section 1: What is Spirit? 10
Chapter 1: God is Spirit 13
Chapter 2: I am a Spirit 18
Chapter 3: Proper Maintenance and Care of Your Spirit 26
Chapter 4: (You) Shalt Surely Die 33

Section 2: Daily Recognition of the Spirit Realm is Called "Prayer" 40
Chapter 5: Everything Starts in the Realm of the Spirit 45
Chapter 6: Spiritual Laws Supersede Natural Laws 49
Chapter 7: Faith Comes from Our Spirits (Hearts) 52
Chapter 8: Words Are Spirit 58
Chapter 9: Imagination is the "Womb" of the Spirit 66
Chapter 10: Your Spirit (Heart) is the Production Chamber of Life 72
Chapter 11: God Communicates with You Through Your Spirit 77
Chapter 12: Your Spirit (Heart): God's Preferred Workplace 84

Section 3: In Our Spirits We Are... 86
Chapter 13: Tapping Into the Mind of God 88
Chapter 14: That Language! That Language! That Language!... 90
Chapter 15: Your Spirit is Your Receiver................................ 93
Chapter 16: "Receiving" Will Never Be the Same Again.. 95
Chapter 17: You Are the Temple... 98

Section 4: Your "Holy of Holies" 102
Chapter 18: The Spirit Realm... 106

Foreword

It may be surprising to learn that your body, although a major part of your life, is only an outer covering. Some call it our "earth suit." With a similar function, astronauts employ a space suit to protect themselves in space. We must have an earth suit to live here on earth. When the suit expires, we must move out into our eternal home. It is the house where your spirit or "inner man" lives. Your eyes can't see the real you inside. They are essentially the windows through which the real you are peering out to see the world.

The public focuses on our physical features, especially on the young and attractive. But our focus on the outer man has left us woefully ignorant of the features, characteristics, and unlimited abilities of our "spirit." I have found this an exciting part of our lives that many know little about. It is the central control system of our being: our heart. The Bible calls it the "hidden man of the heart" (1 Peter 3:4, KJV).

What is "Spirit?"

As we learn more startling revelations about our physical bodies, it is time to learn exciting facts about our spirits. The human body is an amazing creation, but it has known limitations, especially time. The Spirit, however, has no such limitations. It lives on when the body ceases to exist. To me, that's thrilling! Let's delve into a greater understanding of this invisible reality. I haven't heard much teaching on this subject, so I hope to bring some light in this writing.

Everyone, at one time or another, has experienced a gut feeling or a hunch. We were about to do something significant, but we were (what I call) "checked" on the inside, making us feel somewhat uneasy and hesitant. It may have been planning to marry a particular person, purchasing a costly item, or making a major decision about a physical move to another location. Instead, that inner warning was switched on. Perhaps the situation appeared harmless, on the surface but the inner alarm was sounding. This was your spirit sounding off.

Since we're not used to hearing our spirit, its voice can be quite unfamiliar. Yet, on those occasions when it's triggered, we can "hear" it. It's not typically audible, but it can get our attention. I believe this is much more than what we describe as a feeling: it's your "Spirit man". The real you is taking its proper place as your guide and protector from harmful things your mind might allow.

In this writing, I delve into a greater knowledge of the spirit. I want to demystify and simplify this powerful part of our lives. A "hunch" or "gut feeling" is just the tip of the iceberg on an exciting entity in all our lives that beckons more attention.

I've heard the word "spirit" used all my life. It's assumed that we all know what it means. In religious circles, it's used so often that one would think we all know what we're talking about. But usually, we don't.

An apparition, a ghost, or an immaterial being are all quick definitions that immediately define spirit. We have gotten along for many years, not caring what it is, since the material physical world has been the one that seemed to matter most. Everything of a spiritual nature has been relegated to an imaginary realm, mostly a figment of our imagination or personal belief. The word is used in church and around circles dealing with the supernatural, which immediately causes misunderstanding and even fear. The problem is that it's critical, not only that we know, but that we become intimately involved in understanding its birth, growth, upkeep, and empowerment. Why? Because at the core, that is what we are: we are spirit. It is the final frontier.

SECTION 1:
What is Spirit?

Consider the following statements:

1. It is your invisible "inner man," your heart.
2. This is our "natural" state, origin, and actual history.
3. It is your "gut feeling," "a hunch," "a check-in" with what you're about to attempt.
4. It is NOT your mind, will, or emotions.
5. It can be fed and strengthened through feeding and operating in the Word.
6. It comes directly from God and communicates directly with Him.
7. Among its components are intuition, communion, and conscience.
8. It is the production chamber of life.
9. It is our highest existence, like God.
10. It is limitless and eternal.

A "spirit" is a real but invisible, living, active, functioning, and immeasurable life entity inside man's physical body. It is the nonphysical part of a person, regarded as their true self and capable of surviving bodily death and separation from the physical body. It is separated from or leaves the body for its eternal home at death. It is also called the "inner man" and is reputed to be made from the same eternal spiritual substance as God, operating within the body as the control center or "heart." The spirit is composed of immaterial, invisible but real higher-level components, such as the substance of faith, with authority and power to manifest physical things. It consists of a higher dimension and intellect than our everyday function and possesses an accurate knowledge of coming events. It is also the invisible substance from which all visible substances are manifested.

The spirit is the holder, incubator, and production chamber of all unseen things that are in the process of becoming physical manifestations. It is also the vital connector, by common spiritual experience to the "Father" of spirits, God. It is through our spirit entity that we communicate and commune with our Father. It is through our spirit that messages go to Him and vice versa from Him to us. As such, we are not merely physical beings having a spiritual experience with God, but we are spiritual beings having a physical experience for a time on earth, which eventually ends.

CHAPTER 1

God is Spirit

If we believe the Biblical account, our first glimpse of a spirit can be found in the book of the Bible of Gensis. God shows us whose image we are and what kind of being we came from. The Lord was excellent from the start in His breathtakingly creative work. God, a Spirit, is the most prominent personality in the spirit realm. We begin with our focus totally on this Spirit. What better way to commence our observation than to take a closer look at God? We will start our journey off on an exhilarating note. We must fasten our seatbelts as we merely observe what a spirit can do. This Spirit being observed happens to be God.

God is the highest form and most advanced Spirit we know of. We will take care not to be irreverent as we examine Him, but we must look at this eternal Spirit more closely. Similarly, the spirit is like the sun—the center of our universe. It provides both light and heat for our world. The sun is seemingly an unending power source, consisting of gasses igniting, extreme temperatures, and fiery storms.

That is akin to what we observe as we look at God. In fact, Scripture says that God is a Spirit (John 4:24) and the Almighty God. So, let's study Him to understand better what we are.

Our first introduction to a spirit in the Bible is in Genesis. Reading the first chapter is like children watching in awe as this Spirit makes our world. We are fascinated as we hear His words and see through the Scriptural account what He can do. For instance, first, God created light by spoken word. Then, the sun, moon, stars (as lights to the earth's inhabitants), and the earth's atmosphere. Have you read this account and experienced anything close to what is described in the very first chapter of the Bible? My guess is no, and that is okay. Next, God's Spirit hovers over a formless planet and speaks: "Let there be…" Then, things begin their existence.

It is surprising and mind-boggling that God's words produce things, and that the entire universe responds to His words as if it has ears to hear Him. It begs the question: how do trees and oceans hear? As much as I would love to know the answer, any details in the creation process can hold our attention for ages (and has). Astronomy, geology, earth science, quantum physics, etc., were the subjects of our educational process for years. However, this is the highest and best for those who want to know what a spirit is. God is the Spirit at the height of expression who created a physical universe.

Throughout the ages, some have inferred, from this account, that the spirit realm is the mother/creator of the physical world—not vice versa. Another analogy is of a loving parent deciding to build an addition to His house to make room for His children to live nearby. The universe He is making is not for Himself. Instead, it is to be inhabited and managed by someone He has in mind: man. He pays close attention to every detail of the well-thought-out plan. He doesn't need any of what He is creating because He already existed without it. It does, however, seem ideally suited for the prototype image He's about to create. Here are some things we observe about the Creator:

1. Creating physical things is a spiritual expression. God was not content to remain in a solely spiritual realm. If He made all physical things (John 1:2), then all physical things have a spiritual origin. Man has the God-given right and mandate to exercise dominion here (Gen. 1:26). So, the innate desire in all of us to dominate or take dominion is legitimate.

2. Existing in eternity, this Spirit created days or time. He is not subject to it but can move within and without it for His purposes. At our core, we are eternal beings moving within it and, at an appointed date and time, we will pass back into eternity.

3. Creating by speaking was work. So much so that God rested from His labor. Therefore, creating things from words is work. We can attest to that fact in every project we have worked on, from building a house to building a cell phone.

4. God ensured that the things He created were good; this implies that some things cannot be good. Yet, He had a quality standard of excellence.

5. Sight is not the determining factor of what is real for the believer. We don't walk by sight, but we walk by faith. But eventually sight determines whether your faith actions were effective. No visible manifestation after a reasonable period means no real effect. Even faith in the unseen, at some point, must produce its desired effect or the thing for inspection.

6. God created the entire realm, then reproduced Himself or made a new being called man. We also have the ability to reproduce eternal beings through intimacy. Every baby born can grow into an adult who can reproduce and, upon death, will exist eternally somewhere.

7. Spirit capabilities are unlimited. The ability to produce what eyes have not seen or ears have never heard is hereditary. Jesus' statements still ring true today. We should have a God-level of faith. With that, nothing is impossible.

CHAPTER 2

I am a Spirit

I am a growing, developing, maturing spirit. I have a soul, and I live in a body. Another mind-boggling fact is that once I realized I am a spirit-being at my core, I also realized something else wonderful: my history is not limited to the written history of humanity on earth. It's so much more wonderful and, at the same time, tragic. The fact is that as a spirit being, my father is God. He is known as the Father of Spirits (Heb. 12:9). His history is also intimately connected to mine. Following a long line of predecessors, I am related to God. He is a Spirit, an eternal being—but so am I. The tragic part of my history is that my forefather and mother (Adam and Eve) committed high treason against God and lost their first pristine paradise estate. The details of their immediate but lasting demise are found in Genesis 3:7 when they ate the forbidden fruit: "And the eyes of them both were opened, and they knew that they were naked..."

It is believed that the disobedience committed in the Garden of Eden resulted in an immediate disconnection from the glory of God, which was their first covering. After they sinned, they recognized their unclothed bodies. Embarrassingly, they faced the knowledge that their actions had lost them a divine covering and position. Pathetically, they sewed fig leaves together to cover their newly discovered disgrace—their nakedness. We can also infer that the enemy had a hand in their discovery when God remarked, "Who told you that you were naked?" Gen 3:11 NIV. It was obvious to the Lord that the enemy had a say in informing them of their lost innocence.

This account causes us to wonder, "If we are a spirit like God is, what happened?" If we believe the Bible's account of creation, we also believe that we are created in "the image and likeness of God." Our original design is to be like God. Righteousness, authority, love, and power were all in our original design. So, what happened? Why do we feel and experience more unworthy and unrighteous feelings than righteous and worthy ones? Allow me to explain. The Biblical account mentioned in Genesis describes a fall: a violation, a disobedience that resulted in death and separation, namely the death of divinely designed spirits. We were separated from God, our critical source of life. We began our existence in authority over the earth that had been created for us. This was all set up by His edict and was to be followed by the entire creation.

Our design was unique in all creation. The Scriptures describe two actions. First, our bodies were formed from the stuff of earth: our earth suit. This suit possessed the five senses necessary to thrive and survive in the resources and conditions of earth's seasons, climate, and physical conditions. The body was a perfect physical replica of God. Some say it looked like a doll in the exact likeness of God. Second, God breathed into the nostrils the breath of life. Now, we know God does not breathe through lungs like man. So, this exhale of the breath of God was a release of the God-Spirit into man. The miracle of it was the ability of the omnipotent, omniscient, omnipresent God to pour into man the total of his attributes into a finite body.

Section 1: What is a Spirit?

The Scriptures describe Earth as God's footstool and Heaven as His throne. The nanotechnological feat performed at this time was nothing short of absolutely astounding. Man became a "living" soul. Indeed, the term "living soul" is an interesting phrase. Our bodies came from earth, and our breath came from God; together, man became a new creation. The breath that came directly from God was God.

Similarly, combining primary colors, yellow and blue, forms a new color altogether: green. The soul was a new arrival, just like the secondary color green. It was not only created from the earth, body, spirit, or God, it was something new—a living soul.

So, what is the purpose of the soul? It is the only entity on earth with the power of choice. God did not create humanity as robots that follow commands and wishes. Humans are not animals following the impulses of fleshly needs and desires; they are living souls. We are unique. We have the power to make decisions because God thought it was critically important for us to make choices. God is love, therefore, love demands that there should be a choice.

No other beings, not even angelic beings, have this power of choice. Humans are in authority according to the Word of the Almighty God. God placed all of the works of His hands under the rule of man. He would rule the Heavens, and mankind would rule the earth (Psalm 115:16). His edict put everyone and everything on notice that this new creation was the ruler under the Almighty God.

Choices made at the beginning of anything significant set the path and the destiny for the future. At the beginning of the race, Adam needed to set the right things in motion for all that would follow. Unfortunately, when a choice was set before him, whether to believe in God or pursue "knowledge" outside of God, he chose knowledge. His decision was to disobey God and to feed his flesh to enhance his knowledge. It was the choice to strike out on the path of indepen- dence.

Nothing is more abhorrent to God or injurious to man than to follow their own path. Adam and Eve had a lapse in judgment, a simple but critical mistake, a misstep. However, for one so endowed with authority, it was man's choice of high treason that would reshape a creation that was made all "good." This was the shock that shook creation. Man, who was the love of God's heart, rejected the Creator—the Father, and instead chose the counsel of God's archenemy, Satan. Immediately upon their fateful decision, mankind was stripped of its glory. Whatever the covering was that covered their bodies was immediately stripped away. While some say it was the glory of God that kept them unashamed (even though they were naked), His glory was not only their covering but was directly connected to their spirit. That choice thrust them out into a no man's land where they were estranged from God, and Satan could now enter their innermost counsel.

Having chosen knowledge over the spiritual guidance of the Creator, mankind careened off track into an unintended existence. As a direct result, the soul, which is the encasement of the mind, will, and emotions, essentially had achieved a coup and was now in the driver's seat. The fall was not just a mistake; it was a devastating disaster. When God pronounced his future, Adam was told, "You will now live by the sweat of your brow." In other words, a world that would have been your servant will now make you, its servant.

Furthermore, the spirit that would have been his source of knowledge was now rendered dead, comatose by the choice of man to disconnect from God, his life/power source. The best example we have, which is a bit morbid, is like a terminal patient being unplugged from life support: death is often imminent. The fall was immediate and devastating. Mankind fell below the angels, who were our ministering spirits and fell below evil principalities and powers. We even fell below the animals, which could now rise and kill us. It was complete devastation and demotion.

Knowledge, which would have been discerning or downloading from the spirit, was now totally interrupted. With a deceased spirit, man would now have to rely upon his senses and independent mind to determine his path forward. Therefore, using touch, taste, smell, hearing, and sight, he would examine the yet unexplored elements of the earth. Upon receiving physical information, mankind would assess it with his mind, in accordance with past and present experiences, and then record the data. Compared to discerning/down- loading, this deliberate and slow process is how knowledge is acquired today. After centuries of this process, it is evident by the shelves full of recorded data preserved in our universities and learning centers. Sight was the major factor. Accordingly, the unseen, over time, lost its relevance.

Thus, the physical realm became our sole source of reality, and the unseen faded into the realm of make-believe—the imaginary and fantasy. Into this fallen state, we all have been born, spiritually dead, with our souls and bodies in full dysfunction. My hope is that all of mankind will take heed of the Gospel and choose to make Jesus their Lord. That one decision will revive their dead spirits and make them born again. Then, the curse will be broken, their spirits will come alive, and they will respond to God again.

CHAPTER 3

Proper Maintenance and Care of Your Spirit

After Jesus died and redeemed us from our fallen state (2 Cor. 5:17, KJV), the responsibility for maintenance and growth became ours. We are expected to grow up in Him. God is not responsible for what we feed our souls (Eph. 4:15, KJV). Whether we choose "junk food" or nutrition, pornography or promises, movies or messages...the choice is ours.

As stated, each of us has three components: spirit, soul, and body. Our bodies, which contain the five senses (sight, touch, taste, smell, and hearing), are maintained by natural food, exercise, and nutrition. Our souls, which contain our minds, will, and emotions, are fed by intellectual food (i.e., books, classes, schools, universities, etc.). Our spirits contain Godlike elements. Namely,

- Intuition (knowing)
- Communion (constant connection with our Father), and
- Conscience (sense of right and wrong)

How do we feed and maintain our reborn spirits? Let's look at the words of Jesus: "My words are spirit, and they are life" John 6:63 (KJV). Scripture tells us that the Word of God is spirit food. Long ago, He clearly stated, "Man shall not live by bread alone, but by every word that proceeds out of the mouth of God" (Matt. 4:4, KJV). Therefore, our spirits can be fed by the following:

1. **Spirit Leadership** - In order to live on earth, you must have a body to live in. When the body expires, you must leave this earth and go into eternity somewhere. Following the signs of your body are important but it is not the final say. The ultimate authority is the Spirit and its guidance.

2. **Meditating on the Word** - Our minds must be occupied with the things that are real in the realm of the spirit, though these are often unnoticed or even ignored in the natural realm. The images evoked by the

Word (whether healing, instruction, prosperity, or peace) should occupy our thoughts. We should envision what the Word says we have even when it is not yet evident in our natural circumstances. When we do that, we start the process critically necessary for their manifestation.

3. **Practicing the Word** - The Word must be spoken and acted on to release its power. We already know that "Faith without works is dead" (James 2:17, KJV). As the power of the teabag is only released in hot water, the power of the Word is held back until released into our situations and circumstances. This is done through speaking and acting on it.

4. **Making the Word our Top Priority** - Scripture tells us that the Word is God (John 1:1, KJV). It must be given the preeminence in all areas of our lives to effect real change. Though people have often religiously stated, "God's Word always comes to pass," sur- prisingly, this is not always the case. Jesus spoke of this outrageous earthly violation in the parable of the sower (Matt. 13). Although we saw God speak creation into existence and

everything he said came to pass, humankind has had a different experience on earth. Let's consider how Jesus spoke of the sower (farmer) planting seeds (the Word) but getting mixed results. For believers, that is an outrageously unacceptable outcome. No Word from God should ever fail to come to manifestation. But too often, if the Word is not given proper attention or priority in our lives, the roots won't take to the soil.

5. **Instantly Obeying the Voice of Your Spirit** - Many people wonder if the voice they are hearing within is God or themselves. When we feed on God's Word, our spirits develop a voice. Not an audible one, but an inner sensing that begins to guide our lives. If we routinely feed our spirits the Word as they grow, they can be relied on for the right answers and directions. It may be surprising when we look for God's direction, and He remains silent. Why does this happen? It happens when we have grown in the Word and can now be trusted to make the right decisions. In other words, God trusts us and will back up whatever we decide. Paul said on one

occasion, "I speak this by permission and not of commandment" (1 Cor. 7:6, KJV). Paul meant he could decide an important matter, and God would back him.

6. **Praying in the Spirit -** When we pray in tongues (the perfect language given to us by God), we build ourselves up and empower our spirits to do greater things. For instance, we can learn a lot from Eph. 3:16 and Jude 1:20. These Scriptures teach us that just like a bodybuilder gains strength and muscle by repeated trips to the weight room and regular strength- building routines, we can bulk up spiritually by praying in the Spirit. This is a very powerful exercise that, sadly, too few Spirit-filled believers do. Again, this is not up to God but to us. God set the stage and created this simple and enjoyable process for us to access.

You can have as much or as little of the Holy Spirit as you desire. Similarly, a certain amount of forceful wind is required for sailboats to move forward. The problem is not that we don't pray, but sometimes we don't pray in the spirit long enough to get the job done. We are designed to be "strengthened with might by His Spirit in the inner man" (Eph. 3:16, KJV). This verse refers to the might of the Holy Spirit, who is armed with accurate knowledge of our specific individual calling and purpose. The Spirit will give us an utterance to pray regarding His knowledge of our predestination long ago; the Spirit knows every detail.

Prayers directed by the Holy Spirit and prayed to God are perfect. Why? Because they are prayed through our inner man, not through our intellect. Tongues are words that our minds cannot readily understand. That divine language comes through our spirit by the Holy Spirit's direction. We are built up as that holy language prays us out of everything that's not God and into everything God has for us. Our prayers unlock mysteries, hidden truths, and spiritual laws that subdue natural laws like God's Word did initially.

As a result of praying in the Spirit, we "build ourselves up," lining up with God's divine plan. We can then declare, "...all things work together for good to them that love God, to them who are the called according to His purpose" (Rom. 8:28, KJV). This a priceless privilege afforded to every spirit-filled believer. This is not the gift of tongues but tongues for personal edification.

What is "Spirit?"

The amount of time and effort spent on this is up to you. You can do as little or as much as you desire.

CHAPTER 4

(You) Shalt Surely Die

> "But the tree of knowledge of good and evil, thou shalt not eat of it; for in the day that thou eatest thereof thou you shalt surely die. **(You) shalt surely die**" (Gen. 2:17, KJV).
>
> "After Seth was born, Adam lived 800 years and had other sons and daughters. Altogether, Adam lived 930 years, and then he died" (Gen. 5:4-5, NIV).

God warned Adam and Eve about the consequences of eating from the tree in the Garden: "The day **you** eat, **you** will die." The Scriptures above show that Adam lived nine hundred and thirty years before he died. So, what did God mean when He said Adam would die on the day he ate the forbidden fruit? God said, "**You** will certainly die." God spoke directly about His Spirit—the vital component that suffered immediate death when man sinned. God considered Adam a spirit living inside a body when He said, "**You.**" On the day of the violation, the spirit man immediately unplugged from God. It, disconnecting from its life source resulted in death, like a plant pulled out of the ground and a fish pulled out of the water dies from being separated from their life source. Man disconnected from God is dead no matter how long his body is still active and busy. Years later, Adam's body succumbed to the death that had infected his spirit hundreds of years before.

The same one who said, "**You** shall surely die," also spoke through Jesus, saying, "**You** must be born again" (John 3:7). He made it clear to Nicodemus that He wasn't referring to his body but to his spirit. Until we meet Jesus, we are dead, comatose, and inactive in our spirit-man. However, being dead spiritually does not mean we are without a spirit. It means we are dead, like the inhabitants of the Valley of Dry Bones in (Ezekiel 37, NIV): "The hand of the Lord was on me, and he brought me out by the spirit of the Lord and set me in the middle of a valley; it was full of bones. He led me back and forth among them, and I saw a great many bones on the floor of the valley, bones that were very dry. He asked me, "Son of man, can these bones live?"

Section 1: What is a Spirit?

What a lonely existence it must have been for God after Adam and Eve disconnected from Him! He was estranged from the love of his life—man. The period of estrangement would last for centuries. Throughout that time, God had to live among dead men who were active in their bodies and souls but dead in their spirits. It was a devastating truth that the spirit realm, to which they were unable to respond, was the very realm where God lived.

However, that did not mean that there was no activity there. For where God was absent, Satan surely took up residence. Witchcraft, demons, and spiritual pursuits from the dark realm were activated with very little to stop them. To God, it merely meant they were dead. As the centuries passed and their status decreased, men began to be referred to as "souls." At the proper time, the Word of God was preached, and as Paul said in Hebrews 4:12, it divided between soul and spirit, exposing the man's spirit.

The solution to the dilemma described in Ezekiel 37 was for the people to first "Hear the Word of the Lord." Upon hearing His Word, miraculously, the dead bones began to come together: muscles and skin came upon them, life returned, and they stood up as a great army. Can you imagine what it must have meant to break the silence and finally be able to communicate again with man? Oh, how that must have blessed the Lord who had walked alone in the valley (which described the whole earth realm for centuries).

Then, the Lord said something which set the stage for the entrance of the Holy Spirit into our lives. He said, "I will put My Spirit in **you**, and **you** shall live." God's Spirit inside our spirits caused the revival of the ages. And we shall receive power after the Holy Ghost comes upon us (Acts 1:8).

Additionally, we should consider John 3:6, KJV: **"You must be born again."** This statement by Jesus, while understood by us today, went completely over the head of Nicodemus (a Pharisee and a ruler of the Jews). He was thinking naturally at the absurd notion of a man entering again into his mother's womb. Yet, Jesus referred him to the spirit realm, where this was not only possible but expected of anyone who wanted to see the Kingdom. Jesus

Section 1: What is a Spirit?

introduced the "new birth," which was accomplished by believing the Word of God.

Birth by the power of the Word of God had been demonstrated through Abraham and Sarah centuries before, and by the birth of Jesus some thirty years before. Both instances were miraculous. Abraham and Sarah were one hundred and ninety years old, respectively, when their first son, Isaac, was born. Mary was a virgin who conceived from the Word of God and then birthed Jesus. Both were born by faith in the Word of God and not by the natural physical union of a male and female. Needless to say, this was totally amazing. God interrupted Mary's life with her fiancé Joseph to introduce to the world this "new birth" concept. It was a revolutionary new concept of children of God being born by a Word spoken.

Similarly, Mary and Joseph went on to have more children, but Jesus changed everything we knew and brought our inner man into focus. He told Nicodemus, "That which is born of the flesh is flesh; and that which is born of the Spirit is spirit. Marvel not that I said unto thee, Ye must be born again." John 3:6-7 KJV. Jesus was

What is "Spirit?"

referring to the inner man that, up to this time, was dead, having no spiritual life. Peter described it as "Being born again, not of corruptible seed, but of incorruptible, by the word of God, which liveth and abideth forever." 1 Peter 1:23 KJV, once again, the "you" referred to here is the inner man.

Section 1: What is a Spirit?

SECTION 2:
Daily Recognition of the Spirit Realm is Called "Prayer"

The first instance of prayer mentioned in the Bible is "Then men began to call on the name of the Lord" (Gen. 4:26). Fromthat time forward, prayer has been a heavily used resource that reassures us there is more to this life than what we see. Prayer is an admission that the spirit realm exists and that we encounter daily deficiencies that cause us to need its supply desperately. Prayer is the direct road into the realm of the spirit.

Sometimes, this feature is overlooked because prayer is such an integral part of the believer's life. Regular spiritual connection is required to avoid falling apart. Remember that Jesus said, "Men ought always to pray and not to faint" (Luke 18:1, KJV). Some of us pray so often that we don't regard it as a connection to the spirit realm but as our lifeline. Through prayer, we receive Jesus and receive from Jesus. Major happenings that have occurred can be traced back to this activity.

One instance is in the Bible is 2 Kings 6:8-18. This Scripture actually gives us a glimpse into that invisible realm. Surrounded by the enemy intent on ending his prophetic exposure to their secret military plans, Elisha awoke to a terrifying situation. The Assyrian army had traveled by night and surrounded his city. His servant panicked and, in utter hopelessness, said, "Alas, master, what shall we do?" The prophet prayed, "Lord, open his eyes." That prayer opened his servant's eyes to the reality of the superior forces of the spirit realm. Those spiritual forces were a frightening spectacle that brought immediate comfort to his servant. There were a host of forces with fiery chariots surrounding those that were surrounding them. Elisha, no doubt a man who prayed regularly, already knew of this formidable force.

Individuals and groups have become well known when they pray prayers that produce results from another realm. The results were so amazing their names became prominent. The Scripture records: "So Peter was kept in prison, but the church was earnestly praying to God for him. The night before Herod was to bring him to trial, Peter was sleeping between two soldiers, bound with two chains, and sentries stood guard at the entrance. Suddenly, an angel of the Lord appeared, and a light shone in the cell. The chains fell off Peter's wrists. Then the angel told him, "Put on your clothes and sandals." And Peter did so. "Wrap your cloak around you and follow me," the angel told him. Peter followed him out of the prison, but he had no idea that what the angel was doing or was happening; he thought he was seeing a vision. They passed the first and second guards and came to the iron gate leading to the city. It opened for them by itself, and they went through it. When they had walked the length of one street, suddenly, the angel left him. Then Peter came to himself and said, "Now I know without a doubt that the Lord has sent his angel and rescued me from Herod's clutches and from everything the Jewish people were hoping would happen" (Acts 12:5-11, NIV).

Acts chapter 16, the Scripture reiterates: "And at midnight Paul and Silas prayed and sang praises unto God: and the prisoners heard them. And suddenly there was a great earthquake so that the foundations of the prison were shaken: and immediately all the doors were opened, and everyone's bands were loosed" (Acts 16:25-26, KJV). From Scripture, we learn that Jesus was the first to introduce His disciples to prayer. He acknowledged the Father in heaven and the Spirit realm (Matt. 6:9). Furthermore, Jesus taught those He engaged with regularly to follow His advice: "Men ought always to pray and not faint" (Luke 18:1, KJV). This meant recognizing the spirit realm and accessing its unlimited spiritual resources.

CHAPTER 5

Everything Starts in the Realm of the Spirit

Scripture states, "Forever, oh Lord, thy words are settled in heaven" (Ps. 119:89, KJV). This statement implies that the Word of God is established truth in the heavenly realm. In the two realms, we know that God's Word is present and active in the realm of the Spirit. Things occur first in the Spirit or heavenly realm, then manifest in the physical or earthly realm. Understanding the difference is a valuable key to embracing manifestation.

Let's reference the Scriptural example in John 1:1-3 , 14, KJV: "In the beginning was the Word, and the Word was with God, and the Word was God. Vs 14: "And the Word was made flesh, and dwelt among us, full of grace and truth". And the Word was made flesh, and dwelt among us, (and we beheld his glory, the glory as of the only begotten of the Father,) full of grace and truth." Here, we can plainly see that the Word began in spirit form, creating everything, then transforming into flesh. God made all physical things and became a physical being who could be seen with the natural eye (Heb. 2:14). These Scriptures show how things are made or created: they start out as words but transform into physical things over time.

Even as we go about our daily lives, we must think of something (everything) before we physically do it. It starts out in our minds hundreds of times daily before it becomes a physical action or a material thing. Therefore, it would be correct to say thoughts are things in the process of becoming. In an earlier example of this same principle, we read that God told Adam, "On the day that you eat of the forbidden tree, you shall surely die (Gen. 2:17, KJV). The death happened immediately to his spirit, and Adam and Eve discovered their covering was stripped away. However, Adam's physical death did not occur until centuries later. It took time for what had already occurred in the spiritual to manifest in the physical.

Section 2: Daily Recognition of the Spirit Realm is Called "Prayer"

The example of Adam and Eve describes the process and origin of all physical things. Additional Scriptures that support this message includes:

> a. Hebrews 11:3, KJV: "That which is seen was not made by that which appears." Despite the physical reality we function in daily, we are aware, by faith in the Word of God, that there's more than what we see.
>
> b. 2 Cor. 4:18, KJV: "We look not at things which are seen but at things that are unseen," or spiritual things not immediately apparent to the five senses.
>
> c. Eph. 1:3, KJV: God has already blessed us with all spiritual blessings, implying their existence is in the spirit realm.

Equipped with this knowledge, we can approach every endeavor with a confident faith attitude. What we cannot see in the natural has little to no bearing on its existence.

We are often reminded that Jesus was the Lamb of God slain from the foundation of the world (Heb. 13:8, KJV). Additionally, Isaiah 53:5, KJV states that centuries before the crucifixion,

"He was wounded for our transgressions and was bruised for our iniquities..." Faith is also described as "the substance" of things hoped for (Heb. 11:1). It appears that the substance mentioned is spiritual. If we maintain faith and confidence in the power of that substance without doubting, then what we desire in line with God's Word will manifest. Having access to the spiritual realm is a profound advantage to every believer. We have the promise from Jesus that we can shape the unseen with our words and change the seen accordingly. With this in mind, nothing will be impossible for us (Matt. 17:20).

CHAPTER 6

Spiritual Laws Supersede Natural Laws

The laws that govern the spirit realm are more powerful than those that govern the natural physical world. It behooves us to learn spirit laws because what is seen is described as "temporal" or temporary, and what is unseen is described as eternal (2 Cor. 4:18, KJV). Therefore, we must give priority to the unseen.

We have been blessed with a book that pulls back the curtain and exposes what happens behind the scenes of this world. It's your Bible. God has seen fit to grant us not only all spiritual blessings (Eph. 1:3, KJV) but also everything that pertains to life and godliness (2 Pet. 1:3, KJV).

The life of Jesus showed us feats never done before by any man. He walked on water, commanded the storm, cursed the fig tree, raised the dead, fed five thousand, etc. All these miracles demonstrated laws we know very little about. However, they functioned at Jesus' command.

Additionally, Jesus stated we would perform even greater works. His promise is what makes us eager to learn these spiritual laws. Miracles are not magic. They are feats performed from knowledge of spiritual laws that we have been unaware of. What we notice is that these laws supersede natural physical laws. Here are a few:

- The Spirit realm is real—existing regardless of being perceived or thought of
- Words are powerful spiritual forces.
- Faith supersedes time.
- Seeds are the path to supernatural wealth.
- Substance precedes physical manifestation (we must work effectively with the spiritual substance for results)
- Real faith says, "I have it now!"
- Faith is to the spirit what muscles are to the body (it must be exercised and developed)

Section 2: Daily Recognition of the Spirit Realm is Called "Prayer"

- We are not fighting for anything because God has already provided (this is the good fight of faith)

CHAPTER 7

Faith Comes from Our Spirits (Hearts)

Faith is the ultimate thrill in life. To be singled out by God and approached with a promise from Him is the opportunity of a lifetime. Whether that happens as you read His words or from a divine urging inside your inner man, or by His direct statement to you, or by your own choice, faith is the adventure of a lifetime. Faith may require all that you presently possess and your entire life to complete. It will be a challenging experience, but it is worth all the effort expended. No matter what, anyone recognizing this invitation to faith should make it their total life priority.

God wants us to walk with Him daily so we can accomplish our purposes on earth: "For verily I say unto you, that whosoever shall say unto this mountain, be thou removed, and be

Section 2: Daily Recognition of the Spirit Realm is Called "Prayer"

thou cast into the sea, and shall not doubt, **in his heart**, but shall believe that those things which he saith shall come to pass: he shall have whatsoever he saith" (Mark 11:23, KJV). This text teaches us that faith comes from our hearts. Our spirits and our hearts are the same thing. They are spoken of interchangeably in Scripture (1 Pet. 3:4, Rom. 2:29).

No force or power in this world can compare to the force of faith released from our hearts (spirits). It is recorded to be the "substance" of everything that we hope to have in our possession. This physical world surrounds us with circum- stances that are physical facts. They are real to our physical being. We can see, touch, taste, smell, and hear them. They shape our lives. But into our lives also comes Words from God— describing another world beyond the limits of our circumstances. Success in the face of what looks like an utter failure, healing for debilitating illnesses, and protection from hurt, harm, and danger are preached from something called the Gospel or Good News (and the good news it is).

Amid the many forms of misery this life has visited upon us, we are informed from another world, the realm of the spirit. We immediately notice that while our bodies and minds have become used to our physical plight, out of our spirit (heart) comes a lifesaving enrichment called faith. Its appearance is like a light in the darkness, the hope in hopelessness—shaking up the physical status quo. Faith is a spiritual force. Beyond what is provided and even dictated by the five senses, faith emerges as what some call a "sixth sense." Its appearance on the scene changes everything. It immediately becomes the star of the show.

In Hebrews 11:1, AMP, faith is defined as "the assurance (the confirmation, the title deed) of the things [we] hope for, being the proof of things, [we] do not see and the conviction of their reality [faith perceiving as real fact what is not revealed to the senses]." I like to say faith is proof that we own what we cannot see. Nothing can be more thrilling, comforting, and rewarding to our existence on earth. The prospect of transcending our physical limitations and obtaining unheard- of things makes this life worth living. The possibilities engendered by the entrance of this one element into our lives are amazing. It's worth studying and spending time to develop; not just to discover it but to be

Section 2: Daily Recognition of the Spirit Realm is Called "Prayer"

able to wield its force in our normal lives is exhilarating.

No matter the age or season of life, faith is a game changer. The entire Bible is written about people who not only discovered but used their faith to accomplish impossible feats. As we read about the faith of Noah, Abraham, Isaac, Jacob, Joseph, etc., we are motivated to use our faith to experience our own faith adventures. What a godsend is faith! Physical facts for so long have been our master, but faith has come to depose the master and return our lost freedom and authority. Like the slaves of the South upon the Juneteenth proclamation (June 19, 1865), our legal physical confinement has ended. We are free to believe beyond our circumstances. Just like a plane pilot announces over the speaker, "We have reached our cruising altitude. You are now free to move around the cabin," we can also remove limits from our lives.

Faith is an active spiritual force from our inner man or heart. It comes forth and grows stronger daily by hearing the Words of our Father God. It also comes by hearing faith testimonies. God's promises can very well be the only Good News we receive in adverse circumstances. But we find that when we listen, meditate, and imagine what is being said, our faith grows. When faith grows, impossible things become doable. The power of faith takes our lives to a higher level of existence. That doesn't mean the misery ceases immediately or that the opposition ends.

On the contrary, sometimes things get worse immediately before they get better. However, at minimum, the light of faith guides us in the dark places. We can tenaciously grasp faith and hold on for the wild ride ahead. Faith makes any fight a "good" fight because we are designed to win ultimately. Working faith muscles takes us into the spirit realm and gives us experience. Some situations and dilemmas cannot be solved with the technological, physical, and intellectual abilities we presently possess. Faith brings in the promise and power of God to do the impossible. Even if we fall on our faces several times, employing our faith and coming back empty- handed, it is still the only thing of its kind in this life. The only thing that relies and leans on the promises of our unseen Almighty God.

Section 2: Daily Recognition of the Spirit Realm is Called "Prayer"

I have concluded after so many years that I will die using my faith believing in something. The faith journey is ever-illuminating, motivating, and inspiring. Even the hardships it brings are better than anything this natural world offers. And when faith manifests what we desire, we experience what Jesus said: "Until now you have asked nothing in My name. Ask, and you will receive, that your joy may be full." (John 16:24 NKJV)

According to Hebrews 11:3, without faith, we cannot please God. Anyone approaching God must believe that He exists and will reward those who diligently seek Him. It is a costly mistake to achieve great things without developing faith in God. That type of success is misleading. Because there will inevitably come a time when an individual faces a hopeless situation that cannot be solved without it. A terminal disease, an imminent life-threatening event, an unforeseen incalculable urgent need, or danger affecting someone we love...all these challenges require faith, not only in your abilities but in the promises of God. Without faith, your unseen enemy, like a bully, will "take your lunch on the playground," and you will be left wanting.

CHAPTER 8

Words Are Spirit

Jesus said, "My words are Spirit, and they are life" (John 6:63, KJV). Words are living entities. That's an exciting revelation full of new ideas and concepts. The Bible states that "In the beginning was the Word," and it calls the Word God (John 1:1, KJV). God also tells us, "My words have gone out of My mouth and won't return to Me void but will accomplish that which I please" (Isa. 55:10, KJV). Additionally, Psalm 107:20, KJV states, "He sent His Word and healed them", while the writer in Prov. 4:20-22 tells us to pay attention to His words because they provide life and heal every part of the body.

Ultimately, words have much more power than we first imagined. We have used them mainly to communicate with others, either by speaking or writing. However, in the first chapter of the Bible, we are struck by the power of the

Words of our Creator, God Almighty. God used words in a way that was a fantasy to us all. He used them to speak commands to the universe. The surprising thing is that in every utterance from Him, the universe responded with exactly what God commanded. Like a good movie retelling the creation story, reading the Bible and reimagining it seems like a fantasy.

Yet, when Jesus, the Son of God, arrived, He similarly used His words. For example, in Mark 11, Jesus cursed a fig tree. He instructed His disciples "to have faith in God," or a better translation: "Have the faith of God!" The unmistakable implication was that they could perform a measure of what their Father God did at creation. Jesus then informed them that the mountains would respond if they took their words much more seriously and spoke to the mountains. They could have anything they spoke towards. Jesus also inspired their prayer pattern through demonstration. He instructed the disciples to believe they had received what they had prayed for and that they would receive it in return. This recorded instruction took words of command and words in prayer to a more powerful and confident level.

What is "Spirit?"

Though initially surprising, the concept had already been demonstrated in the Old Testament. For instance, when he was old and had lost his eyesight, Isaac instructed his son Esau to hunt, catch, and prepare a special "savory meat" for him. He planned to give Esau his words of blessing before he passed away. The story detailed how

Rebecca, Isaac's wife, overheard his words and secretly told Jacob to disguise himself. Then, Rebecca prepared savory meat for Isaac to step in and receive his father's blessing instead. Who knew an older man's words could mean so much?

Deception was utilized so that words could be spoken over Jacob. In the end, the scheme was successful, and Jacob received the blessing spoken over him instead of his brother. When Esau arrived later and heard that Jacob had stolen his blessing, he cried out in utter anguish and begged his father to bless him. However, he was informed that the blessing had already been spoken, and he was too late. From that day forward, Esau swore that he would kill Jacob. Many have wondered why Issac didn't speak another blessing over Esau. The reason is that he believed with all his heart that his words would come to pass.

Another example of verbal impact can be found in Joshua's Biblical account. After enduring forty years of delay in the journey to the Promised Land, he finally engaged his enemy and defeated them in a pitched battle. However, there was one problem: daylight was ending, and the victory wasn't complete. Fearing that too many enemies would escape by nightfall, Joshua spoke words with bold audacity. He said, "...in the sight of Israel, Sun, stand thou still upon Gibeon; and thou, Moon, in the valley of Ajalon" (Joshua 10:12, KJV). Contrary to belief, according to the Biblical account, what Joshua spoke came to pass. There was never such a day like it: the sun and moon stood still until his army soundly defeated the enemy. This was not God but a man speaking— expecting his words to come to pass.

Additionally, we have all heard of the shepherd boy, David, who defeated the giant Goliath with a sling. His words are worth noting as well: "You've come to me with a sword and with a spear, but I've come to you in the name of the Lord of Hosts, the God of the armies of Israel whom you have defied. This day, I will take your head off your shoulders and feed your armies to the birds of the air and beasts of the fields." David believed with all his heart that his words were coming to pass. It would have been a bloody suicide to fight this giant if he didn't believe in what he was saying.

Another example of the power of the tongue can be found within God. Look at how He regards his words: "For as the rain cometh down, and the snow from heaven, and returneth not thither, but watereth the earth, and maketh it bring forth and bud, that it may give seed to the sower, and bread to the eater: so shall My Word be that goeth forth out of My mouth: it shall not return unto Me void, but it shall accomplish that which I please, and it shall prosper in the thing whereto I sent it" (Isa. 55:10-11, KJV). As the children of God, we should note how our Father speaks about His words and mimic Him. It is a good idea to practice saying this about our words also.

Jesus said, "...every idle word that men shall speak, they shall give account thereof in the day of judgment. For by thy words thou shalt be justified, and by thy words thou shalt be condemned" (Matt. 12:36-37, KJV). The word "idle" means inoperative, non-working, or empty. This takes our words to another level, thrusting upon us a greater responsibility when we speak. Words are not just for communication; they are also a major component in our power to *create*, just like our Father God.

How can we raise our words to the level of creating? Proverbs 4:20-22 KJV gives simple but powerful instructions for this. It states: "My son, attend to my words; incline thine ear to my sayings. Keep them in the midst of thine heart.

For they are life unto those that find them and health to all their flesh." The instructions are as follows:

1. Pay undivided attention to God's Word.
2. Take time to hear His Word often.
3. Memorize and meditate on His Word.
4. His Words are life and medicine to every part of your body.

What is "Spirit?"

Jesus stated, "If you abide in me and let my words abide in you do, you shall ask what you will, and it shall be done unto you" (John 15:7, KJV).

If we desire our words to rise to the creation level, we must first spend quality time in God's Words, as described above. This process builds faith and confidence. After doing this for a while, an exciting promise is in effect: your words will come to pass. We already know this is true because Jesus revealed to us the spiritual nature of our words. He said, "My words are Spirit, and they are life." Therefore, words have the attributes of Spirit; they can be sent forth to accomplish an intended mission. Have you ever thought that your words were capable of such? If not, reconsider Jesus' Words. He said that we can speak in such a way that whatever we say will come to pass, and nothing will be impossible for us. The prospect of this happening in my life is nothing short of thrilling. No matter what season of life you are in, this is both inspiring and motivating.

Further confirmation is located in the first chapter of John. John stated that the Word was *with* God, which meant it could be dispatched

Section 2: Daily Recognition of the Spirit Realm is Called "Prayer"

on a mission. He also said that the Word *was* God. That means that God has made Himself so accessible that He can be in your heart and be spoken through your lips in any situation. What a powerful truth! John 1:14 details the culmination of years of waiting and anticipating. Again, John stated that the Word was made flesh. The manifestation of what was spoken throughout centuries had become a physical fact. This is what all believers live for: our words (prayers, commands, decrees, etc.) to manifest and become physical things.

CHAPTER 9

Imagination is the "Womb" of the Spirit

The first process of manifestation is this: we must first conceive a thing in our imagination before it can be brought to pass. Whatever we desire, we are required to meditate (imagine) day and night so that we will receive it. Imagination and meditation are the same.

God has given man a feature that is so exciting it's hard to take it in. Our imagination is limitless— it is the place where we are king. It's been said that "whatever you can imagine, you can have," and vice versa (if you cannot imagine it, you cannot have it). To be healed, we must see ourselves healed. The believer must see it. Without that inner sighting, there is no guarantee of what is desired. Remember what Jesus said: "Believe you receive when you pray, and you shall have it" (Mark 11:24, KJV). Man is

Section 2: Daily Recognition of the Spirit Realm is Called "Prayer"

powerless in prayer without believing or seeing the desired outcome inwardly.

Who would have dreamed that we have a part in the outcome of prayer? We always thought only God handles prayer. It bears repeating that prayer is powerless without believing (or seeing ourselves with what we prayed for). Taking time to see ourselves with the desired outcome is meditation. For instance, the Lord instructed Joshua that to have success, he must be involved in this exercise day and night. He plainly expressed to Joshua that by doing this, he would be the one, not God, making his way prosperous. The principle came from God, so ultimately, He gets the real credit. However, to involve a mistake-prone and sin-prone man in this wonderful exercise is just too wonderful. When we meditate and see ourselves with the answer, we are co-creating using the principles left us by God for our glory.

As we walk more in our new creation, we cannot allow the same pictures we allowed before. There must be a clean sweep of the old way. God is now putting His principles in our minds. As such, our imagination will have to be guarded and protected. We no longer have the luxury of being open to any thought or image. We have a divine purpose and are on assignment to manifest what God called us to do. This is not just a choice. It is a weapon against the strategies of our enemy. If, as stated above, our imagination is the womb of the spirit, we dare not allow anything we don't desire to be placed there.

Likewise, the Apostle Paul revealed that the weapons of our warfare are not carnal or physical. Still, they are mighty for the pulling down of strongholds. Though anything can be considered a stronghold, Ed Silvoso identifies it as a mindset impregnated with hopelessness that causes an individual to accept as unchangeable that which he knows is contrary to the word and will of God. In Scripture, we learn that "Casting down imaginations, and every high thing that exalteth itself against the knowledge of God and bringing into captivity every thought to the obedience of Christ" (2 Cor. 10:5, KJV). Keeping the right image or picture in our imagination is key to manifesting our desires. If we are not just servants but actual sons of God, we need to know how to shape the unseen to change the seen. Shaping the unseen is our privilege as well as our responsibility. We have been given keys to the Kingdom. We must

Section 2: Daily Recognition of the Spirit Realm is Called "Prayer"

be vigilant if we know that our imagination is the womb of the spirit.

Many people have quoted Scriptures that promise them healing for their bodies. Yet, they have never really seen themselves healed in their imagination. It takes time and effort to remember such a picture when the nurses are busily taking vital signs, the medical machines are noisily beeping, and the doctors are assessing your physical diagnosis. However, somehow, we must keep healing planted "in the womb of our reborn spirit." Somehow, we must strive to maintain a healthy "pregnant" spirit for as long as necessary. In other words, no baby will be born if there is no baby in the womb. I hope you get the analogy.

Along the same lines, Joshua was instructed to keep the divine image produced by God's Words firmly planted in his mind (meditating). If he meditated day and night on God's Words, he was promised the success he would need going into harm's way (Joshua 1:8, KJV). He would need a powerful faith foundation since he replaced the iconic, larger-than-life leader, Moses, and fulfilled the centuries-long dream of entering the promised land. Keeping the right image in the womb of the spirit accomplished that. Bible history records he successfully routed fearsome giants and conquered the land promised by God.

Another valuable feature of meditation is revelation: what God reveals to the one meditating on His Word. Too many believers leave it to the speaker on Sunday to give them revelations from God's Word. They don't realize it, but they're forfeiting a great blessing. Once we hear a Word from the Lord, whether preached, taught, or read. It's time to meditate.

Meditation is to the spirit what digestion is to the physical body. We all have our favorite meals; we enjoy the aroma as they are prepared and the taste when served. Although taste draws us to our favorite meal, taste is not the primary purpose. Nutrition is. However, it takes time for the nutrients of our food to get into our bodies. That usually happens a little while after we taste and digest it. Meditation on God's Word is similar. Once we hear it, no matter how anointed, we should recognize we only got the taste. It will take time for meditation to get the nutrients (revelation) into our spirit. Major leaders in the faith have described meditation

Section 2: Daily Recognition of the Spirit Realm is Called "Prayer"

as the key to their success and progress in the ministry. The message spoken by a minister can be powerful. But nothing replaces the personal clarity and revelation that comes with meditation.

CHAPTER 10

Your Spirit (Heart) is the Production Chamber of Life

Proverbs 4:23, KJV declares: "Keep your heart with all diligence. Out of it flows the issues of life." Our hearts (spirits) are our production chambers given by God's design. The entire Kingdom is operated by sowing (planting) seeds into our hearts' production chamber (soil). The process is as follows: a man plants the seed, which is God's Word, His promises, and His revelation, into the soil of his heart. It is incubated there by memo- rization, meditation, and believing. Like natural soil, it needs no instruction from there. Then, He allows the growth process of germination and maturation. He doesn't know how things will happen because the seed is hidden. But he is confident that what he desires is taking place.

Section 2: Daily Recognition of the Spirit Realm is Called "Prayer"

The due season may be relatively short or after some time has elapsed. After a period, the sower should expect the stages of growth. First, the blade, then the ear, then the full corn in the ear. Next, it's harvest time. In other words, the expected promises manifest. Overall, this is what successful sowing and reaping looks like. We should all be more actively involved in this process. It is a great, unlimited blessing of being like our Father God.

There is another scenario that many of us (to our disappointment) are more familiar with. Matthew 13:3-8, KJV states: "And He spake many things unto them in parables, saying, 'Behold, a sower went forth to sow; and when he sowed, some seeds fell by the wayside, and the fowls came and devoured them up: some fell upon stony places, where they had not much earth: and forthwith they sprung up because they had no deepness of earth: and when the sun was up, they were scorched; and because they had no root, they withered away. And some fell among thorns. These thorns sprung up and choked them, but others fell into good ground and brought forth fruit, some a hundredfold, some sixtyfold, some thirtyfold."

In this example, the sower planted the seed of the Word of God into his soil (heart, spirit) but experienced scattered results. As the sower planted the Word, some fell by the wayside and were eaten up. This means the Word was not understood, and its powerful potential was disregarded. So, the enemy strategically snatched it away. Some fell on stony ground, were scorched, and shriveled up. Here, the Word was received with great joy and celebration but never planted deep enough to withstand the heat of tests. Some were planted in soil full of thorns and choked. This occurs when the Word must compete with other priorities. The end result is that it doesn't produce. However, the seed which fell on good ground, where the Word was believed and received, brought forth a bountiful harvest. That's what we desire when we diligently keep our hearts, knowing that it is the production chamber of life.

Durable results can only occur if we follow the process of sowing seed into good ground, watching over it, nurturing it, and, in due season, receiving the harvest. Though some seek after anointed services, gifted speakers, and ministries for impartation, miracles in these platforms are often short-lived. Taking this

Section 2: Daily Recognition of the Spirit Realm is Called "Prayer"

approach is like having your battery run out of power and relying on a jump start without addressing the need for a freshly charged battery. People who engage in such behavior resign themselves to short-term effects.

Additionally, miracles can sometimes seem like "faith accidents." In those times, we were joyous over the miracle but didn't know how to repeat it when needed again. It appears the Lord has placed into our hands a process that can be learned, repeated, and relied upon for supernatural results. But we must be aware that the supernatural doesn't always mean spectacular. Some things can only come forth by planting seeds and following the prescribed process for harvest. This is a method we can teach to anyone.

Another critical factor is that, for believers, there is an expectation for growth. Like parents expect their children to grow and develop abilities to solve issues, God's children likely build up their faith to possess and keep the blessings that belong to them over time. **"It is critical to understand that you can only keep that which you have built your faith level up strong enough to keep."** For example, suppose you receive your healing in a wonderfully anointed healing service. In that case, it's not wise to think miracles last regardless. Every believer is expected to build his/her faith to the point that if challenged, they can survive and thrive through the challenge. Faith needs to be built up to believe beyond what we see or feel. God's Word, not our feelings or experience, is the determining factor.

And sometimes, that may require getting up when that's the last thing we feel like doing. We are expected to apply faith principles and not lapse back into doubt.

CHAPTER 11

God Communicates with You Through Your Spirit

> "The spirit of man is the candle of the Lord..."
> - Prov. 20:27, KJV
>
> "And the very God of peace sanctify you wholly, and I pray God your whole spirit and soul and body be preserved blameless unto the coming of our Lord Jesus Christ."
> - 1 Thes. 5:23 (KJV)

We interact within the physical realm since our physical bodies function within five senses (seeing, hearing, touching, tasting, and smelling). With our soul (mind, will, and emotions), we interact with the intellectual realm. With our spirits (intuition, communion, and conscience), we interact with the spirit realm. Every individual is responsible for nurturing and developing each of these entities. How we address the needs and requirements of each determines our quality of life both now and eternally.

Although each area feeds information to us, there is only one that God has chosen to communicate with us: our spirit.

In the past, we have read about God's display of frightening power, thundering, lightning, and shaking the earth. This was during the time of Moses when the commandments were given. People were frightened by God's presence and feared death if they wandered too close to Him. However, these were physical displays of God's presence designed for people who were spiritually dead. Seeing these spectacular physical manifestations caused people to be afraid even to say His name casually. It affected both their bodies and their souls to experience these amazing displays.

The prophet Elijah put forth a bold challenge to prove the real God. He said, "The god that answers by fire, let him be God" (1 Kings 18:24, KJV). God answered the challenge with unusually potent fire released from heaven that totally consumed the altar. It would appear that this was God's chosen way of making Himself known to His people. Yet, sometime later, as Elijah ran to escape Jezebel's anger, we see a different approach from God. Hiding in a cave,

Section 2: Daily Recognition of the Spirit Realm is Called "Prayer"

Elijah experiences a wind so strong it breaks rocks in pieces. After the wind, an earthquake occurred; then, a fire. However, throughout these powerful displays, God did not communicate with Elijah. Instead, God waited until after the fire to use a still, small voice. This was the approach God took to talk to Elijah; this was His pretext for teaching.

Although some are more familiar with and accustomed to physical displays, this is not God's chosen way of communicating with us. He has chosen to lead us by the spirit of man. Who doesn't love a physical manifestation of God's power? We seek that daily as we should. But we are spirit beings, and at some point, we must exercise the designed function of our inner man to hear from God.

I have witnessed believers putting out "a fleece" like the one described in the time of Gideon (Judges 6:37, KJV). This Biblical account occurred during a period when people were spiritually dead. In those times, it may have been necessary to rely on the physical displays of God to make decisions on important issues. God worked with the shortcomings of men back then and answered them accordingly.

However, times have changed. Present day, if anyone attempts to put out a fleece, they should realize this fact: that approach limits God to the *sense* realm and doesn't grow your faith properly. It is an unreliable action. Satan, "the god of this world," can manipulate physical elements to cause havoc. God has a better way, and His way is more personal through the spirit of man.

Similarly, Prov. 3:5 reads, "Trust in the Lord with all thine heart; and lean not unto thine own understanding." Much of the knowledge accu- mulated over the centuries has been what is called "sense knowledge." It was amassed under the fall of man with very little input from the Spirit. A much higher level is "revelation knowledge," which comes from the Spirit realm. Sense knowledge can be very helpful in the daily affairs of our lives. We learn it in schools and universities all over the country. Yet, it is limited to the experience of the five senses and the unregenerated mind of man.

The intellectual realm has many avenues of learning and pursuits of knowledge beneficial to us. Learning trades and the diligent pursuit of careers can reap sizable rewards. However, compared to the things that we can access in the spirit realm, that self-seeking approach is child's play. Instead, God takes things that appear foolish to the natural mind and confounds the wise. Those of us who have arrived at the limitations of the knowledge of man have come to realize that there is a vast difference between a *good* idea and a *God* idea. During times of inevitable challenges that leave us perplexed in this life, believers are blessed to rely on trusting the Lord with our hearts (spirit). We no longer lean on our own understanding. From here, knowledge transitions from an exercise of the mind to a condition of our spirit. We get a "knowing" in our spirit even though our minds are still wanting.

Since Proverbs 20:27 has instructed us of God's chosen way to communicate, it's time to become better acquainted with it. Some have already become accustomed to this method. A "hunch," gut feeling, or a "check" inwardly are all parts of this inner communication. Believers often speak of an "inner witness" in which sensing of agreement from the Holy Spirit happens.

To demonstrate, God some time ago moved His entire operation to the inside of man. We see this truth in Jesus' speech: "The Kingdom of God is within you" (Luke 17:21, KJV). Our help is no longer expected to come from the hills outside us or from the rain coming down on us. The Greater One is now on the inside. We've prayed for rain, and now there's a well on the inside from which we must operate.

We must activate the inner witness by taking time to hear the voice inside of us. In doing so, this may require more waiting on the Lord. Yet, getting the correct guidance is well worth the wait. God will first communicate to us through His Word. In His Word, we learn His patterns, likes, dislikes, and character. Through His Word, He pulls back the curtain on unseen heavenly realities—exciting blessings that belong to the born-again believer. When we learn God's patterns through His Word, we embrace His primary form of communication. The more we hear and meditate on God's Word, the stronger we become spiritually. Fear will wane, and faith will increase to another level.

As we become used to the patterns of God's Word, we learn what His will is and what it isn't.

Section 2: Daily Recognition of the Spirit Realm is Called "Prayer"

After a time of learning, our spirit man can guide us because we have fed it a steady diet of God. In return, divine instructions and guidance will pour out. God's Word is a living substance. Spending time in it brings life to our spirit man as He speaks to us in our affairs. Likewise, anytime God wants to communicate with us, He speaks through our spirit directly to us. As a result, our inner man (spirit) can now be relied upon for accuracy. Over time, the question, "Was that me, or was that God?" will become more recognizable as we learn to listen to God and communicate with Him. That "hunch," the "check" in your spirit, or that "gut feeling," becomes the leading of the Lord.

CHAPTER 12

Your Spirit (Heart): God's Preferred Workplace

> *"And shall put my spirit in you, and ye shall live."*
> *- Ezek. 37:14, KJV)*
>
> *"Man looks on the outward appearance, but the Lord looks on the heart."*
> *- 1 Sam. 16:7, KJV*
>
> *"That he would grant you according to the riches of his glory, to be strengthened with might by his Spirit in the inner man."*
> *- Eph. 3:16, KJV*

God has always been concerned about the real *you*, your spirit or inner man, the *you* that no one can see that's living inside your body. He doesn't look on the outside for the real *you*. He does all His work on the inside of you. Man can only look outwardly, but God knows that the only place His work can be effective is in your heart (spirit). He leaves us with our bodies and souls so that we can align them with what He

Section 2: Daily Recognition of the Spirit Realm is Called "Prayer"

does in our hearts. Therefore, like the Scripture says, "I urge you, brothers and sisters, in view of God's mercy, to offer your bodies as a living sacrifice, holy and pleasing to God—this is your true and proper worship. Do not conform to the pattern of this world but be transformed by the renewing of your mind" (Rom. 12:1-2, NIV).

The spirit or heart of man is God's focus and destination, but the body and soul (mind, will, and emotions) are ours. The limitless capacity of our spirit to contain the work of God is nothing short of astounding. In the spirit, God has done a work that leaves us breathless. Thank God it's unseen but not unreal. It's in our imagination, but it's not imaginary. It's fantastic but definitely not fantasy. It's spiritual, which means the process of its manifestation is underway.

We should always remember: "What manner of love the Father hath bestowed upon us, that we should be called the sons of God...beloved, now are we the sons of God, and it doth not yet appear what we shall be; but we know that when he shall appear, we shall be like him..." (1 John 3:1- 2, KJV).

SECTION 3:
In Our Spirits We Are...

As we have demonstrated that all things have their beginning in the realm of the Spirit, let's look at what the Lord has already accomplished there. In our spirits, we are:

1. No longer servants but born-again sons of God (Gal. 4:7)
2. Heirs (Gal. 4:7)
3. New creatures (2 Cor. 5:17)
4. Qualified, delivered, and translated into the Kingdom (Col. 1:12)
5. Reconciled, righteous, and justified (Rom. 5:18-21)
6. Resurrected from among the dead (Eph 2:1)
7. Raised up and seated with Christ in heavenly places (Eph. 2:6)
8. Entrusted with keys to the Kingdom (Matt. 16:9, Luke 12:32)
9. Restored to authority (Luke 10:19, Rom. 5:17)
10. Restored to our wealthy place (Ps. 66:12, 2 Cor. 8:9)

CHAPTER 13

Tapping Into the Mind of God

> *"'For My thoughts are not your thoughts, neither are your ways My ways,' saith the Lord. 'For as the heavens are higher than the earth, so are My ways higher than your ways and My thoughts than your thoughts'"*
> - Isa. 55:8-9, KJV
>
> "But we have the mind of Christ."
> - 1 Cor. 2:16, KJV

Another awesome benefit given to us needs a little more explanation. Before I explain it, there is an exercise that every spirit-filled believer can engage in, which ends the condition described below. It stands to reason that God's thoughts and ways will always be so much higher than ours. The way to tap into His thoughts and ways is to pray in the Spirit.

The Scriptures have informed us that we can speak God's hidden wisdom mysteriously through the Holy Spirit's language. God knows

His own mind and has blessed us with a language that taps into His glorious, boundless thoughts. So, we should no longer be satisfied not knowing what's on God's mind. What eyes haven't seen, and ears have never heard is now being revealed by praying in the Holy Spirit with tongues (1 Cor. 2:10-12, 14:2, KJV).

When we spend time praying in the Spirit, revelation is the result. We begin to see things and know things never revealed or known to man. This was one of the keys to the revelatory things Paul wrote. He said, "I thank God, I speak in tongues more than all of you" (1 Cor. 14:18, NIV). Instead of confessing our ignorance in situations, we should include this spiritual benefit in our daily speech. We have the mind of Christ! Whatever we confess with our mouths, believe in our hearts (spirits) according to His Word will be our salvation.

CHAPTER 14

That Language! That Language! That Language!

> "But we speak the wisdom of God in a mystery, even the hidden wisdom, which God ordained before the world unto our glory."
> - 1 Cor. 2:7, KJV
>
> "For with stammering lips and another tongue will he speak to this people? To whom he said this is the rest wherewith ye may cause the weary to rest, and this is the refreshing, yet they would not hear."
> - Isaiah 28:11-12, KJV.

Nothing can compare to the blessing bestowed upon our inner man, being equipped with a language neither our natural minds nor the enemy can sabotage. The language that accompanied the Holy Ghost outpouring on the day of Pentecost in Acts 2 was a supernatural manifestation. Never before had such a thing occurred. Jesus didn't talk much about it in His teachings, but after His resurrection, He said it would be a sign among believers (Mark 16:17).

Who would have expected that "stammering lips" and this peculiar language would play such a critical role in the ongoing life of believers? It was so different, and some thought the people had gotten hold of a new wine. Though they weren't far from the truth in that way of thinking, it was a new approach and had an intoxicating or otherworldly effect. In time, those who received this manifestation learned it would charge up their lives with power from above. It would also allow them to receive mysteries or hidden truths from heaven in their otherwise ordinary lives.

Although this seemed like foolish, unintelligible babble on the surface, this was God's new way of getting critical revelation to his people. It bypassed both natural thinking and the mental interference of the enemy. God's children were required to go past their minds and human understanding and trust in God by speaking the syllables inspired by the Holy Spirit. By engaging in this heavenly language, believers could expect to experience what "eyes had not seen, nor ears heard..." (1 Cor. 2:9, KJV).

What is "Spirit?"

Through this language, God's people discovered that God would reveal everything He gave freely. They would no longer be limited to the statement, "His thoughts are not our thoughts, and neither are His ways our ways" (Isaiah 55:8, KJV). To their amazement, through this holy language, they could say, "We have the mind of Christ" (1 Cor. 2:16 KJV). When we spend time in that language, we download hidden truths from God that He wants us to discover and disclose to others. Accordingly, the results are mighty revelations.

CHAPTER 15

Your Spirit is Your Receiver

The spirit is where we receive things from the Lord. We can receive things from the Lord in word form, while our physical bodies have no idea anything happened. In other words, the spirit is OUR RECEIVER. Proverbs 20:27 tells us that messages, words, promises, and healings can only be held in the heart or spirit of man. The capacity of our spirit to be the container of our dreams is evident in the fact that God chooses to place it there. Even Jesus stated, "The kingdom of God cometh not with observation: neither shall they say, Lo here! or, lo there! for, behold, the kingdom of God is within you." Luke 17:21 This means that we are host to the entire Kingdom. We have always been designed to live from the inside out.

We are bigger inside than out. God lives on the inside of us because greater is He who is within you, transcending the laws that govern matter (1 John 4:4, KJV). In the spirit realm, two things can occupy the same space at the exact same time. We are strengthened with might by God's Spirit in(side) our inner man. *Wow!* The almighty God is inside of us. This almost begs the question, how much capacity do we have to contain Him? It is far beyond awesome! When we really get that revelation, we will transform into totally different people.

CHAPTER 16

"Receiving" Will Never Be the Same Again.

We have already discussed that everything occurs first in the spirit realm and then appears in the physical realm. This is how prophets can predict future events with clarity and accuracy. They are very aware of the two-part process and are very sensitive to its activity. Put another way, prophets can read tomorrow's headlines today. Knowing about this process also gives every believer an advantage. Again, it can help us shape the unseen and change the seen. This is a powerful concept! With this in mind, as we focus on the inner man, receiving from God will never be the same again.

Likewise, most believers pray and wait for manifestation. Once we see it, we rejoice because we feel our prayer has been answered. Much to the contrary, that is not how we receive when we focus on our inner man. Let's look at these Scriptures:

- "Everyone that asks receives." - Matt. 7:8, KJV
- "What things soever you desire when you pray, believe you receive them, and you shall have them." - Mark 11:24, KJV
- "This is the confidence that we have in Him that if we ask anything according to His will, He hears us. And if we know that He hears us, whatsoever we ask, we know that we have the petition that we desired of Him." - 1 John 5:14-15, KJV

These Scriptures speak of praying and petitioning as confident exercises. Asking is receiving. If you've lived any length of time on this earth, you know this is not our usual experience when we pray.

However, what if manifestation depended upon believing you already received what you prayed for? What if the fulfillment of your petition was totally based upon whether you actually believed you already possessed what you requested? When we are aware of the capacity of our inner man to receive what we request, everything changes. When we claim complete ownership from the time we pray without regard for whether we see it physically or not, we have entered another realm: faith ownership. Our inner man *receives* when we pray. What we ask is already owned on the inside. Our eyes are of little use to us during this time. It's with the eyes of faith that we see that we have what we've asked. This is the fight of faith.

Do you realize the shift that is occurring in our prayer of petition? We are moving from living in the "effect" to living in the "cause." Instead of being bound to having things happen *to* us, we can now have things happen *for* us and *by* us. As divine beings related to God, as His sons and daughters, we are in the creative class. Jesus said nothing would be impossible for us when we believe. We begin to participate in their creation as we believe fervently in the things we desire. That may sound a bit far-fetched, but it is true, it is a pattern that is developing. Remember what Jesus said: "*whatsoever* you desire" (Mark 11:24, KJV). Therefore, God will bless our petitions when we believe we already own what we have prayed about.

CHAPTER 17

You Are the Temple

When God gave Moses specific instructions for building the Tabernacle, He divided them into three parts: the outer court, the holy place, and the mysterious unseen Holy of Holies. We are called "God's temple" because the three distinct parts of the temple are our true image: spirit, soul, and body. On the outside, our outer court represents our physical bodies with the five senses. With our bodies, we touch the earth or the physical realm. The Holy Place, with its table of showbread and candlesticks, is typical of our souls. Our mind, will, and emotions are contained here. This part of us interacts with the intellectual realm and its man-made ideations, ideologies, and feelings.

Yet, the Holy of Holies is where God spoke to Moses, between the cherubim or angels, which overshadowed the mercy seat. It was separated by a thick curtain and forbidden to anyone but

Section 3: In Our Spirits We Are...

the high priest, who once a year came to offer sacrifice for himself and the sins of the people. This is our focus because it relates profoundly to our spirit or inner man. For so long, it was a hidden place of mystery and fear. It is reported that they would tie a rope around the high priest, put bells on his robe, and listen as he did his duties. If the bells stopped, that possibly meant that he had sinned and had died. If that occurred, the people feared too much to venture in but could pull him out by the rope if necessary. Regardless, this is the place where God spoke to Moses.

Likewise, now inside our innermost being, our spirit, is where God speaks to us. Our spirit possesses intuition, revelation, communion, and conscience. Again, God does not choose to communicate with us through our minds or physical bodies. Instead, He clearly showed man's design to Israel and the world. His work is astounding. He created a holy place— the center of life for His people, Israel. To them, the temple was the place where God lived. With its sacred instruments, holy rituals, and dedicated sancti- fied priests, that place was everyone's priority. It was the house of God on earth. Yet, to everyone's surprise, centuries later, the Apostle

Paul revealed that after its construction, this would become a picture of the design of man.

At the crucifixion, the curtain separating the sacred Holy of Holies from the Holy Place was mysteriously and miraculously torn from top to bottom. This was to signify that God was no longer content to dwell in a man-made building. With the atonement accomplished by shedding the blood of the Lamb of God, He would now dwell inside man. This was a feat like no one had ever dreamed of. It was astounding, mind-blowing, incredible, inconceivable, and *true*. The prophecies of Joel, Ezekiel, and others would now be fulfilled. God's Spirit would now be poured out upon flesh and live inside of man (Joel 2:28, Ezek. 37:14).

This monumental moment ushered in the current era of the Holy Ghost—the time when God himself would revive, raise, and inhabit man's dead spirit. There was never a time before when God lived inside man. Now, God dealt directly with man's inner being from the inside. Even Adam, who was made in the image of God, could not relate to this experience. But on the day of Pentecost, as is described in Acts, Chapter 2, there was a sound of a rushing mighty wind. It was the sound that after centuries of dwelling outside of man, God would now be closer than ever before.

This moment would change all reference points. Help would no longer be considered "coming from the hills." They would no longer have to pray for something from the *outside*, like rain. The power was now on the *inside*. Not rain, but a well. As Jesus prophesied, "Out of your belly shall flow rivers..." (John 7:38, KJV). The focus shift from outside to inside still has some men trying to wrap their minds around this major trans- formation. Despite the change, God's people embraced the joy, deliverance, guidance, and Son of God living inside of them (Col. 1:27). Victorious life was now designed to be lived from the inside out.

SECTION 4:
Your "Holy of Holies"

Do you know you now have a "Holy of Holies" inside you? Just like in ancient times, we have a sacred sanctuary, a private place. Back then, only the high priest was allowed to go in. Now, this restricted area is once again reserved for you and God alone. This is where you commune with God—a real communion. You enjoy your union with Him as a "like spirit," spending time in His presence, taking on His divine attributes, and learning His voice and ways. There is where we express our deep desires, and He assures us there are no limits or boundaries to His love for us.

In times of communion with God, we are strengthened mightily by His Spirit in the inner man (Eph.3:16). We begin to get an idea of what we have already overcome because the Greater One forever lives in us (1 Jo. 4:4). There is no greater experience than having an audience with God. Though we cannot easily get an audience with public officials, we can have an immediate appointment with God without waiting.

Since God is always available, many people have cried out for Him to answer them with a physical manifestation. Some had placed "fleeces" before Him like Gideon did to get answers but later learned their efforts were unreliable (Judges 6:37-40). These people were attempting to get God to move within the realm of the five senses. However, they failed to realize that the adversary has the ability to intervene and interrupt within the five senses. We cannot forget that the enemy is called "the god of this world" (2 Cor. 4:4, KJV).

When teaching spiritual maturity, God will not answer the believer in the way of the world. Instead, He willingly suffers the risk of being called nonexistent, even if it angers or frustrates the individuals desperately trying to connect. The only reliable place for God to speak to His people is through their spirits. Prov. 20:27 declares, "The spirit of man is the **candle of the Lord** searching all the inward parts of the belly." In other words, our spirit is the main place we receive from God. What we receive from God in our spirit is so natural to us it can best be described as a "hunch." When our conscience is activated, it's an uneasy feeling about an action we have already taken or are about to take (although our mind may feel like it's okay). Other times, our souls will permit as "allowable" what our spirits condemn as out of bounds.

CHAPTER 18

The Spirit Realm

In conclusion, let's take a moment to review everything we've learned about the Spirit realm:

1. It's our origin, our normal state—like God (Gen. 1:26, Psalm 82:6)
2. It's real—existing regardless of being perceived or thought of (Heb. 11:6)
3. It's limitless—the bounty already exists NOW (Mark 10:30)
4. It reminds us that confident asking is RECEIVING (Matt. 7:8, 1 Jo. 5:14)
5. It proves that "having" is owning before physical evidence (Mark 11:24)
6. It helps us work the "substance" (Heb. 11:1)
7. It teaches that manifestation is a definable process (Prov. 4:20-22, Mark 4:26-29)

8. It produces inspiration.
9. It encourages meditation.
10. It encourages revelation.
11. It encourages application.
12. It helps us with the manifestation.
13. It reminds us that thoughts are things (2 Cor. 10:1-4)
14. It supersedes physical laws: "I will restore the years..." (Joel 2:28)
15. It has an unlimited capacity to house God and Kingdom (Luke 17:21)

What is "Spirit?"

www.ingramcontent.com/pod-product-compliance
Lightning Source LLC
Chambersburg PA
CBHW050440010526
44118CB00013B/1606